I Don't Want to Wear a Mask!

Written by Tiffany Turner

Illustrated by Natalia Cano

Copyright © 2020 by Tiffany Turner
All rights reserved.

This book or any portion thereof may not be reproduced or used in any manner whatsoever without the express written permission of the publisher except for the use of brief excerpts for review purposes.

First Published in 2020

Shadowcat Publishing

Printed in the USA

Dedicated to:
My Parents. I've become the person I am today through your guidance. Thank you.

Albert was starting Kindergarten soon. He was looking forward to it until something terrible happened. A virus called COVID19 spread throughout the world. Schools had been shut down including his preschool.

He had to stay at home and only talk to his friends on his computer screen. His teacher talked to him through online classes. They even had to miss their preschool graduation.

On the last day of preschool, his teacher said to the class, "You'll enjoy Kindergarten so much. You'll officially be full-time school kids now. I'll miss you in preschool."

"I'll miss you too," Albert said to his teacher.

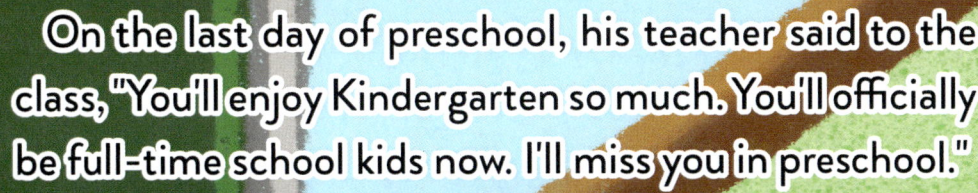

"But remember, it will be important to do as your new Kindergarten teacher says, and things will be different than they were in preschool. Most of all, you'll have to wear a mask."

"I don't want to wear a mask!" exclaimed Albert.

He ran into his room and lay on his bed. "I don't want to wear a mask." He said it over and over until his mother noticed he had run away from his online class session.

She sat next to him on the bed, stroking his back in soft circles. "Why don't you want to wear a mask?"

"Because things are so different. We can't see our friends. We can't play outside. And most of all, I don't want to wear a mask."

"But Albert, it's important." Albert's mom kept talking in her soothing voice. "Sometimes we have to do things we don't want to do to help others. Wearing a mask will help protect others at school. It will protect teachers, your friends, and their families."

"But I don't want to wear a mask," he said into the pillow.

"It will help stop the virus from going into other people they meet. From the postal worker, to the grocery clerk, to the nice librarian you see each week. They'll all be safe because of you."

"Really?" asked Albert.

"Yes. It will keep all of their families safe. They won't bring the virus home to them if you wear a mask." She patted him on the back. "You'll also have to wash your hands more at school. It would be something a superhero would do to help save everyone around him."

Albert turned to face his mother. "You mean I could be a superhero?"

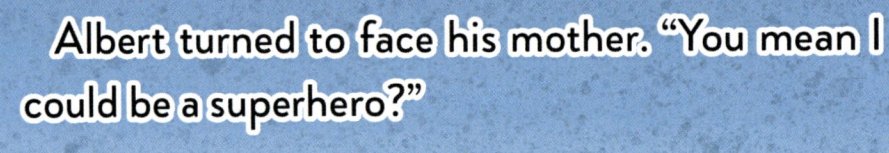

She winked at him. "You can even choose the color of mask if you like. Or we can look for a fun pattern. We can even get you several, one for each day of the week."

"I can be a superhero wearing a mask?" Albert started to think about all the different things he could do in a mask. He could be a ninja. Or he could be a pirate. Or he could be a secret agent. Each day, he could be a new kind of superhero with a different mask.

Albert sniffed. "Okay, Mom. I'll wear a mask if you can help me pick them out."

His mom leaned forward, grabbing him into a hug. "That's it. Remember, you can save the world now. Keep everyone safe by wearing a mask, washing your hands, and staying safely away from others. It will be a lot different at school now than it was before. But together, I think we can make it work. Does that sound okay?"

Albert nodded his head. "I think I can do that, Mom."

"Good, then. Let's go pick out some masks," she said, wrapping him up in a hug.

It was the first day of school for little Albert. He was so excited to start his first day of Kindergarten. Now, he could be a true superhero.

He felt great walking into the classroom and meeting his new friends because they were all wearing masks too. They were all superheroes together.

Made in the USA
Middletown, DE
23 April 2021